Investing

Mastering The Art Of Wealth" Is A Crucial Guide For
Individuals Seeking To Navigate The Complex And Ever
Changing Investment Landscape In Today's Financial
Landscape

(Offering Valuable Insights And Advice For Both Novice)

Casey Mcgrath

TABLE OF CONTENT

Terms Explaining The Value Of An Option..........1

Mentors Aren't Deities. 17

Bonds, Equities, And Liquid Resources 35

Getting By In The New Economy And Growing
....55

Additional Things To Think About When
Investing...76

Flipping Houses: The Second Season...................91

What Goals Do Investments Have?......................94

Terms Explaining The Value Of An Option

We do not characterise the performance of an option as flat, up, or down. Such a description needs to be revised. Alternatively, we can specify the version in one of three ways.

In the money: An option with inherent value is referred to as being in the capital. An option contract is considered to be in the money whenever the strike price and the stock price in the stock market favour the contract owner.

Out of the money: When there is no chance at all of making money by exercising an option, it is said to be out of the money. This indicates that,

1

compared to the general securities market, selling stocks and shares at the strike price is far less profitable or financially feasible. Therefore, if the strike price of a call option exceeds the cost of the stock, we say that the choice is out of the money.

At the money: The strike price and stock price can occasionally be roughly equal. When this occurs, we refer to the option as being at the capital.

Exchange-traded funds: what are they?

You can think of an exchange-traded fund as a mutual fund that doesn't have a fund management and trades on a stock exchange. Although the expense ratios for exchange-traded funds are typically low, an exchange-traded fund still needs management because the entity that manages them still needs to acquire and sell stocks and other securities. Exchange-traded funds are available for buy and sell on stock exchanges without any loading or additional fees. Therefore, exchange-traded funds do not have formal minimum investment restrictions, although many mutual funds will have minimum investment requirements that could be as high as $5,000. Thus, the price of a single share of stock will be the minimal investment required.

To fulfil any investing requirement, exchange-traded funds are also offered. Exchange-traded funds have grown at an exponential rate over the last 20 years, so you can find a fund to achieve any investing objective, including dividend-paying funds. These are also provided by a diverse range of companies so that you can find exchange-traded funds with varying entry costs. In other words, you can invest in various funds with similar stated objectives but with differing share prices, which makes it simpler for you to make an investment. Along with looking for funds that pay dividends, you can also examine each fund's performance data to discover how the fund has historically returned on investment.

Exchange-traded funds, then, are mutual funds minus all the extra baggage. We should have clarified that mutual funds trade just once a day following the closure of the market. Therefore, you can go to your mutual fund provider and place an order for additional shares in the fund; the transaction will be completed that evening. Exchange-traded funds, on the other hand, are listed on the stock market, so you can purchase and sell shares of them whenever you please, just like any other stock.

Acquiring Stock

Let's say you have decided to buy stocks. For the typical individual, such as yourself and me, a stock brokerage handles this.

In the stock market, a brokerage serves as a go-between for individual buyers and sellers. This was a convoluted process years ago. From the beginning to the end of a single transaction, it would frequently require a personal relationship with a broker and multiple phone calls.

These days, it's considerably easier. I use the internet services offered by Charles Schwab, where there are no transaction fees and everything is fully automated. Schwab does not charge a tiny transaction fee for each purchase or sale, in contrast to many other online brokerages. It's easy to grasp, straightforward, and effective.

Later on in the book, I'll go into greater detail about this technique. We'll go over a comprehensive example, complete with screenshots, of how to buy your first stock.

Companies: Public vs. Private

What distinguishes a private corporation from a public one? Every business starts out as a private one. This indicates that the founders own all of the company and that no stock is available for purchase by the general public.

Frequently, after a business has been around for a while and is doing reasonably well, it will opt to go public by means of an IPO. The company benefits from this since an IPO enables them to raise capital through investor interest in buying their shares.

Businesses frequently utilise the funds raised from an initial public offering (IPO) for internal expansion, which includes developing new goods, constructing new facilities, employing staff, etc.

An officiating bank sets the price for a company's stock. This bank examines the institutional investors' desire for the company's stock as well as the fundamental worth of the business. The initial price of the stock increases with the number of investors who wish to own a portion of the company, and vice versa.

A company can start competing as soon as it is made available to the public on a stock exchange. Purchase and vend as much as desired!

And these are only the fundamentals. There are literally dozens of various stock investment techniques available in this market, along with a plethora of intricate alternatives for both purchasing and selling stocks. When it comes to assessing firms, financial pundits have generated an infinite amount of complexity, and trying to determine the state of the market right now will make your head spin.

Remember Munger's previous statement? "Our ideas are too simple, which is why they haven't spread faster."

Because it keeps its business growing, financial pundits and news outlets have created a certain character around the stock market that is challenging and convoluted. What option do we have if investing in the market is too risky and difficult for average people to generate decent returns? Surely, we can go to the "experts" and trust in their financial knowledge.

I am an unabashed follower of the Warren Buffett investing approach, also known as "value investing." Value investing allows people to keep their agency and faith in the stock market while taking control of their financial future.

I should warn you upfront that value investing is by no means a get-rich-quick tactic before we get too technical. But if you take the plunge now, you'll be able to leave the nine-to-five grind considerably sooner than if you wait until you're sixty-five.

I'll Always Remember My First Time

The subprime crisis of 2008. I was still investing even though I was young, reckless, and free at the time. The US real estate market was at the time spiralling into an unprecedented vortex. The banks were forced to foreclose on the homes of millions of American households because they were unable to make their mortgage payments.

Prices decrease when there are more sellers. Supply and demand are at play. Real estate, as is commonly known, is an investment; one could lose money if values decline.

Lehman Brothers, a prominent US bank, filed for bankruptcy. Like in any financial crisis, there was a collapse in the stock market. My financial portfolio, which was already limited before the crisis, was at its lowest point at the age of twenty at the time.

I told my banker over the phone to sell every stock in my portfolio since I may potentially lose 50% of its worth. I made a foolish, emotional, and immature decision as a rookie, and the main reason was that I wasn't ready for such a rejection.

I had yet to evaluate my own level of risk and volatility tolerance. Looking back, that was actually pretty low.

I was devastated by the loss. When I sold my investments, the hypothetical loss we had discussed materialised.

Simultaneously, because it happened when I was still young, it was the best investing lesson I have ever learned. Fortunately, it was also a very inexpensive lesson. It gave me the composure to face the 2020 stock market catastrophe and the self-awareness to determine how much volatility I could handle. In keeping with my quarterly commitment to rebalance, I not only did not sell my stocks during the peak of the 2020 crisis, but I also took advantage of the low prices to purchase even more of the stock ETF.

Realise that there is no "right" or "wrong" investment; rather, the best kind of investment is one that fits your personality and doesn't cause you to break out in cold sweats. 50/50 is the ideal ratio for you, or it's 90/10 or 70/30. You should choose alternative financial avenues if your character isn't suited for stock investing, even if it involves putting in more overtime than you had anticipated.

The purpose of the lazy approach is to push you, gauge your level of risk tolerance, help you determine the best allocation for your requirements, and help you grow numb to distracting noises and harsh outside influences.

Remarkably, you can begin investing modestly and gradually raise your amount. Your initial portfolio can have a level allocation of 50/50 at the beginning, and you can determine that you will only add to the stock until it increases to 70%.

You can buy things with savings that you might not be able to afford at the moment.

If you're like most children, your needs and wants won't be fully met by the money you earn from jobs like babysitting, chores, or allowances. This could lead you to think that some things are expensive, but that's not always the case; if you wait and keep saving money for your purchase, you can afford them.

It's through saving that "no, you can't" becomes "you can, but later."

Savings can help you avoid financial difficulties in an emergency.

When creating a budget, most people do a decent job of factoring in regular costs such as rent or vehicle insurance. Their proficiency in handling unanticipated expenditures, like unexpected job loss or unpaid medical bills, needs to be improved. If you have these kinds of expenses, you can borrow money, but it could be a better idea because lenders usually charge you costs, such as interest. You can use the money you've saved to pay off debt if you preserve any.

Savings encourage independence.

Recognise it. You don't want your parents controlling every aspect of your life. (Well done for being typical!) If you save money, you can make purchases without depending on your parents or anyone else. This in no way suggests that their viewpoint is no longer respected. It means that you can become more independent by taking on some of their financial obligations and carrying them yourself.

Future financial independence is increased through saving.

Sometimes, saving money means making a smaller purchase. For instance, the lender will typically offer you a better, less expensive deal if you have saved up and are able to pay cash at a vehicle dealership or make a higher down payment on a home since they will associate these actions with lower risk.

Your options are increased since you can use the money you would not have to spend in these situations to purchase other items you may need or want.

Putting extra money in your pocket by saving could also bring you more freedom. For instance, the bank will only provide you a small amount based on your balance if

Mentors Aren't Deities.

Only some have the good fortune to study in a graduate programme under a recognised guru who also serves as their mentor. However, Warren Buffett did precisely that when he visited Columbia, the home of David Dodd and Benjamin Graham, the influential pair who had authored the book on value investing. Buffett was soon thrown into a world he considered to be paradise. For Buffett, studying businesses, reading everything he could get his hands on, and getting to spend time in classrooms debating and conversing with Graham was akin to returning home. While he was there, he took in everything he could and formed relationships with Graham and other like-minded students that continued well after class.

Graham provided the foundation for his concept, which is to always purchase with a margin of safety. These three phrases, "margin of safety," are what Buffett believes to be the "cornerstone of successful investing," as you have already read in the section about risk. Graham also taught Buffett the fundamentals of value investing. He gained knowledge about computing intrinsic value, which involves estimating a company's present value as well as its future value. He became knowledgeable about the whims of the market, particularly about Mr. Market, the figure Graham frequently discussed, and all of his corresponding irrationality. Buffett looked up to Ben Graham, and he probably still does. Without Graham's foundation, Buffett would never have been the successful investor that he is today. However, Buffett gradually began to change his perspective when he started his investment profession and learned more about the business world and what made companies successful.

Although he was still firmly in the value camp, he started to consider more qualitative factors rather than just the quantitative ones that Graham was concentrating on. He even noted in one of his shareholder letters that the value versus growth debate is meaningless because both are necessary for a company to be a profitable investment. Graham's focus was solely on the financial figures, regardless of the company's operations, management composition, or prospects. Even though he was adamant that purchasing a stock equated to buying a portion of a real operating business, he was also more interested in calculating the total value of a company and its market value. This was the investment "cigar butt" school, as you were previously taught. But Buffett was meant to be more than just a connoisseur of cigar butts. He was supposed to realise that everything that is incredibly inexpensive is inherently bad.

Buffett was initially made aware of this fact by Charlie Munger. When Munger made his investment, he took more into account. He also disliked paying too much for firms, but the main reason he didn't purchase companies was that their asking prices were much lower than their true worth. That did not persuade him to buy. He thought that being well-managed and possessing a competitive edge was important. He also held the opinion that, in order to have a stake in a potentially lucrative venture, you occasionally had to pay a little bit more than you would have preferred. Munger said that rather than searching for obnoxious old cigar butts to take a final puff from, "Why don't we look for great businesses run by good folks and buy those?" Buffett had never heard of this before. He gradually realised that Munger was correct and that he could build a comprehensive investment philosophy that was exclusive to him by fusing the best aspects of Graham with a few more qualitative elements.

Investment Mutual Funds

These funds don't need to be company stock shares. Securities such as bonds and stocks are among the assets in which you can invest. Money managers oversee mutual funds. They put together a particular kind of asset and make sure the fund is diversified by holding bonds, stocks, and securities.

Depending on how many units they own, investors purchase shares in the fund and split any profits or losses.

ETFs, or exchange-traded funds, are traded on stock exchanges in a manner akin to that of stocks. Bonds, commodities, and supplies will all be included in the group of funds that make up an ETF. ETFs will generally follow stock indices. ETFs share several characteristics with mutual funds, including the fact that the fund's efficient management determines the net asset value.

Four things are available for purchase and sale on the market, as you can see. Bonds are a reasonably simple long-term investment to comprehend. Stocks, on the other hand, are your best bet if you desire a hands-off, active involvement in the market. If you are not seeking hands-on investing, professional management of mutual funds and exchange-traded funds (ETFs) is preferable. Pay attention to these funds and exit the market if you need to make money.

If you choose to use these products, you must have faith in the mutual fund or ETF fund manager.

Mutual funds comprise a large portion of the 401(k) investments. In reality, several firms provide the S&P 500 mutual fund, which makes it simple for you to invest in big, reliable corporations.

These are also the primary investing choices that stock exchanges provide. If you feel that the stock market doesn't offer enough "security" for your investments, you have other investment options.

Tape Reading and Supply and Demand

So, what exactly does tape reading entail, and how do supply and demand affect stocks? A tape, then, is a condensed account of every deal that has taken place that day. It displays to the public the cost, volume, and duration of each agreement. Many penny stock traders find that it is an effective method for assessing the movements that take place during the day, as well as for observing and recognising any swings and possible openings.

A trade is typically referred to as a print when it is completed and represents the entire number of shares that were purchased and sold. It is both the actual price at which the claim was sold and the moment the sale really occurred.

Most trades happen at the asking price, which is represented by the colour green. The exchange will appear in red if it does, however, happen at a bid price; if it actually occurs between the two, it will appear in white. While this may seem like little, it is wise to avoid drawing any incorrect conclusions about the data, particularly regarding the colour codes, since red is typically associated with negativity, particularly in the financial sector.

Identifying the distinct trading patterns that are taking place is one method you can take advantage of. For instance, you may see the volume, the offers and bids that are being made, and the rate at which the shares are changing.

Restrictions on Short Sales (SSR)

You can think about using this short-selling tactic, but it's only sometimes advised. Still, it's always helpful to understand how it operates. For instance, the SSR will essentially be activated to limit the quantity of trading with that stock till the conclusion of the following trading day if it declines by 10% or more from the previous day's closing.

This rule is applicable to all stocks, regardless of the exchange where they are traded, although it can significantly affect dealers of penny stocks. In day trading, falls more than 10% can be quite advantageous, but this is heavily controlled by restrictions imposed ten years ago. It is not advisable to engage in short selling; nonetheless, if you are thinking about it, be aware that the limitations will be a significant drawback. It might be difficult for you to turn a profit on this one.

Additionally, you may use real money to buy some of these enjoyable second-life items if you don't know how to manufacture them. Real cash. It has its type of money to spend in the second life realm. The Linden dollar is the name of it. These dollars are convertible into US dollars. The exchange rate does, however, occasionally rise and fall. The money supply determines the exchange rate. Additionally, the money supply is affected by the ratio of new to premium accounts as well as ongoing adjustments to second-life bonuses and stipends.

The linden dollar is worth more in the second life world than the money we earn in this one. In the game, there are various methods to earn Linden dollars. You can operate a business in the real world or take a virtual job, similar to job advertisements. To gain money, you can design things, open a restaurant where patrons can purchase food, establish a hangout for members, introduce monopoly games and other forms of gambling. Additionally, you will earn roughly L$3 if you spend fifteen minutes or more sitting in a camping chair. Further, three Linden dollars will be valued in US cents.

The Avatar represents you you make. You have complete control over how your Avatar looks. You can create a stunning avatar appearance editor to help you express yourself in the best possible light. You could add an avatar's head, body, clothing, and body attachment. You have the option of selecting an avatar that depicts a goddess, an animal, or a vampire. Your choice of Avatar reveals a great deal about your character. To those you interact with in the Second Life virtual environment, your generated Avatar represents who you are. When creating your Avatar, keep in mind that it provides a window into your personality and way of thinking.

You have the freedom to become anyone you wish to be in the second life and to follow your passions, aspirations, and objectives. Some users interpret this as an opportunity to gain as much money as possible; others interpret it as a licence to shoot other users; still, others interpret it as a licence to pilot a spacecraft; yet more interpret it as a licence to attend parties, go on adventures, and live worry-free. Additionally, some users utilise it as a space to hone their artistic or creative talents. For example, if you're an artist or maker, Second Life allows you to capture images and make movies. Additionally, there are prizes for the top filmmakers and photographers.

For the most part, the virtual world is a great way to meet new people and form friendships. It's a lovely spot to play with other people. You can communicate with someone you don't know or will never meet in real life in second life. Both parties agreed upon everything that transpired between two people in the hereafter. Rules are in place.

You cannot make fun of or disparage someone because of their gender, ethnicity, sexual orientation, or religion; instead, you must tolerate them. Harassing someone is wrong. In the virtual world, harassment can take various forms. Stop if you see that something you've said or done has offended someone.

Never hit out at another member. When in an area that has been designated as safe, do not shoot, push, or shove a second-life inhabitant. An emblem representing the safe state will appear above the bar.

This provides us with a glimpse of what the metaverse will look like, even though it will be more intense and distinct from the virtual world of Second Life. They can earn money in the second life world just like we can, and they can adopt any avatar personality they choose. In the second life world, they have their digital currency. They can enjoy themselves greatly and accomplish more than they could in real life. The inhabitants also created the houses, the land, the sea, and the animals.

A prime example of the metaverse, second life gave everyone the opportunity to explore their abilities and become the person they want to be. It was suggested that individuals would be able to trade, earn money, make investments, and purchase land in the metaverse. Their destiny is in their hands. They have the power to choose what will happen to them and what they wish not to occur in their lifetimes.

The following are available as virtual properties:

Characters, digital games, and merchandise for sale

Purchase a video game online by downloading it to your computer or through a digital retailer like the PlayStation store or e-shop that is connected to your platform of choice. It will not be able to be sold. Certain firms only permit you to play the material and not to own their product. So, a digital licence is what you purchased. However, there are a few things you may do to earn money from the games on your own.

For example, you may sell off different game goods for money. Some people have made money from selling previously used characters from games like Warcraft games via third-party markets. However, this is not acceptable.

Selling an in-game item for the game's currency is an additional method. You can sell at the auction house or trading area. On the digital marketplace for your game, you may exchange it for cash.

Selling e-books, music, or pictures

If you own the rights to your items, it is simpler to find digital copies of your work than something made by someone else, like a video game. One option is to use an online marketplace, such as eBay or Amazon, which has a sizable consumer base. They can easily handle tasks like processing refunds and making payments without having to worry about it. In order to keep track of all of your earnings, you can also build a website for your digital business or use invoices as a bill of sale.

Technique Eight: eBay Sales

Selling items you have lying around that you have yet to use on eBay is an additional choice.

● You must first compile a list. To list your goods for sale on eBay, you must provide information about it. All of the essential details a buyer could require, including a photo, price, description, mode of payment, and other pertinent data, are included in listings. With eBay's Sell Your Item form, you can see how to create and submit an item listing step-by-step.

Select a section. You can use the "What are you selling?" Search Box to help you classify your product. Select "Start selling" from the menu.

Since buyers frequently use titles to narrow their searches, creating a compelling title and description is essential. Your titles must, therefore, be intriguing enough to draw readers in. For your reports to be effective, they need to be clear, contain all the necessary information, and present a positive picture of your product. Make sure that all of the text and images you use for your advertisements are encrypted and contain HTTPS content.

Add information about the item. Providing item details in a category is a better way to make an object stand out. For certain types, item details are not available.

A nice picture provides additional details about your products to your customers. By utilising eBay Picture Services, you may enhance and incorporate your images.

Selecting the most advantageous auction or fixed-price format enables you to choose the one that best fits your needs and makes you a successful seller.

● Choose a price: To offer yourself some flexibility and control over your price, set the starting bid, establish a reserve price, and consider using buy-it-now options.

● A listing's duration can be set between one and ten days. eBay postings often expire after seven days.

● Provide shipping information. Clearly state your delivery options and pickup locations. When estimating how long it will take you to process a product after you receive money, don't forget to factor in delivery time. Customers can more accurately predict how long they will have to wait for their purchase, thanks to this.

● Decide on and establish a return policy. I advise you to set a return policy in order to give your clients a better purchasing experience. That being said, even if you state in your item description that you do not accept returns, you must nonetheless make this apparent. If you don't include a return policy in your ad, eBay will select one for you.

● Enhance your listings with specific additions. Listing your improvements—bold, highlight, and border, for example—may improve the appearance of your product.

● When creating an item, don't forget to add just the price, title, and description. You can spend less time answering clients' questions if you provide them with additional details about your return policy, delivery options, and payment options.

Examine your data. An early draught of your product page will be visible to you. Use the "Edit listing" option to fix any issues you find.

Bonds, Equities, And Liquid Resources

You will encounter a few new terms as you proceed through the investing process. It's crucial to look up unfamiliar words and phrases as you meet them to avoid becoming really confused. A basic Google search phrase typically works. Ask the financial advisor to explain whatever they are saying if you need help understanding them. A good financial advisor will act in this manner without hesitation. When you begin investing in passive funds, you will hear some terms spoken here.

Stocks: This type of investing enables you to own a portion of a specific firm. As an illustration, you own a piece of Coca-Cola if you hold shares in the corporation. Since you will receive a part of the company's profits, you are referred to as a shareholder. Additionally, you can decide on the company's course. Purchasing stocks allows investors to increase their capital. Those who purchased such stock participate in the earnings when the value of that particular share rises. Your first investment was $150 if you bought ten shares of a stock at $15 a share. Your investment is now worth $200. Therefore, you will make $50 if the price rises to $20 a share. Naturally, a shareholder may lose money if share values decline. Via the stock exchange, stocks can be bought separately or as a component of a fund, such as an index or exchange-traded fund (ETF).

Bonds: Another name for bonds is fixed-income securities. Bonds are issued to investors by governments or private companies when they require funds for specific initiatives, to maintain ongoing operations, or to refinance debt. In essence, these bonds are loans that will have interest paid on them. This implies that when you buy bonds, An investor is required to hold onto a bond on the security date in order to sell it. To turn a profit, they can sell them at any time. Compared to stocks, bonds are significantly safer because you won't lose money. You also lose out on the same potential for rewards as a result. Bonds and stocks are combined in the majority of funds and portfolio models. Bonds are less common in the higher risk portfolios than equities.

Assets with high liquidity are those that are simple to turn into cash. Regular checking and savings accounts, for instance, are regarded as liquid as you can withdraw money from them right away. Since they cannot be easily changed from real estate, gold, silver, and different investment portfolios into cash for legal tender, these items are not regarded as liquid assets. Because they are the primary source of money utilised for financial obligations and transactions, liquid assets are crucial for both individual investors and enterprises.

As you proceed, many more terms related to money will appear. It truly is a language unto itself.

1.3 What is a cryptocurrency?

One type of digital money that can be used as a payment mechanism or as a form of payment is cryptocurrency. Since their transactions are virtual, they process, secure, and verify them using encryption.

No central entity, like a reserve bank, controls Bitcoin or other cryptocurrencies. In a blockchain system, for example, they cannot be edited or otherwise altered until certain conditions are met.

Also has a side project with cryptocurrencies. Nakamoto intended to develop an electronic cash system that would enable transactions without the need for a central authority, as opposed to inventing a form of money.

The network is more secure because it is decentralised, meaning there isn't a central server where operations are managed or a regulatory body. Every transaction made on a decentralised network like Bitcoin is accessible to all users. Public keys of the sender and the recipient are also contained in every transaction file.

1.3.1 O The Advantages of Digital Currency

Cryptocurrency may be bought with just a button click anywhere in the world. Anybody with internet access is able to purchase and own whatever digital currency they like. Ownership of cryptocurrencies and transaction processes will become less complicated in the future.

Virtual currencies contribute to their increasing appeal. Unlike other electronic currency settlement systems, cryptocurrency payments can be made instantly.

Due to their cheaper transaction costs, cryptocurrencies are becoming more and more popular as a means of international money transfers. Due to the various expenses involved, using different financial portals for money transfers may be expensive.

The fact that customers can make purchases with cryptocurrencies without disclosing their identity is another aspect that has contributed to their popularity. There are altcoinswhose main objective is to protect the privacy of transaction data.

1.3.2 Cons of Cryptocurrency

The intricacy of cryptocurrencies has led to resistance against their usage by some countries and organisations. A major hindrance to the expansion of digital currencies is the widespread ignorance regarding their use.

This, together with the fact that a transaction cannot be undone once it has been completed, is a significant disadvantage for a lot of people. Asking the beneficiary for a refund is the only course of action available in the event that a transaction goes wrong. There is little that can be done if the person who received the money from improper marketing refuses to return it.

The biggest negative aspect that has damaged the public's perception of cryptocurrencies is volatility. The influence of volatility on a coin's value might take time to understand or manage.

Facts versus Markets

A notable value investor is someone who knows a great deal more about specific firms and their stock performance than they do about the stock market. While everyone else is raving about how the cryptocurrency market is a terrific place to invest, value investors are aware of the specific businesses that have established themselves as successful ventures and those that have outstanding branding teams. This value investor is not concerned with what a broker or the news may say. They concentrate on real individuals in the business or sector they are interested in, as well as the rivals. Put otherwise, the value investor must deal with the reality.

However, the same factors also have an impact on a company's actual intrinsic value, particularly when taking into account changes in capital expenses and increases in the value of alternative investments. Indeed, you should pay close attention to the markets, especially when looking at them in the long run. On the other hand, swings without underlying principles should be disregarded. Years may pass before you see significant returns, so be ready for that. It is not your responsibility to forecast changes in the market.

To Be Clear, What Is Not Value Investing

Conservative and value investing are not synonymous. The goal of traditional investing is to minimise risk while making every effort to optimise short-term gains. , are examples of conventional investing. Nevertheless, not all of these investments meet the value standards, which include: • Considerable intrinsic worth; • Predictable and stable returns.

Put differently, not all value investments are conservative; rather, not all traditional investments also happen to be value investments.

Furthermore, while not all value investments are long-term, the majority of them are. As a matter of fact, not all long-term investments are worthwhile. The duration of business cycles is decreasing these days, particularly as technology keeps altering how we conduct business.

Making sure you're ready for any potential shift in the markets or firms you're watching is a straightforward yet effective strategy to handle this problem. When the time comes, you ought to be prepared to short them. Value investment can be profitable for a year.

Value investing is about more than just a cheap cost relative to earnings. Food producers, banks, and oil businesses are often reliable sources of lower-than-market price-to-earnings ratios, although this only sometimes translates into a profitable investment. The earnings may not be long-term sustainable. When determining whether to invest at a good price, the P/E ratio is undoubtedly important, but it's not the only factor you should research.

Despite how these two have been compared, value investing is not the inverse of growth investing. It would be absurd to argue otherwise because growth is a major component of the value. The expansion of a company is what brings in the desired profit. A company's potential for growth, not merely its current level of operations or assets, is what determines its worth. To value, one must grow.

You will discover that cheap is relative when it comes to value investing. Purchasing businesses at or below their true appraised value serves a purpose beyond securing a great deal: it provides a buffer of safety.

Why does the safety margin matter? Since valuing firms is both an art and a science. It's an art since there are other less obvious aspects of a firm to take into account before determining its value, and it's a science in that there is a method behind it. Because of this, valuing a business can be inaccurate; therefore, having a margin of safety is one strategy to address this imprecision. Put differently, and there is an opportunity for error in the unlikely event that things don't turn out the way you had anticipated.

This is not to say that value investors only search for stocks that have seen consistent declines in price over 52 weeks. You should likely wait to buy a stock if it has been falling for so long because the company may be experiencing major problems. It involves examining how the market price compares to the true value of the business.

Additionally, value investors have been known to purchase or go long even after companies have been trading at 52-week highs for an excessive amount of time. However, in these cases, their analysis indicates that the current market price is not yet at the assessed fee. Even though this isn't always the case, remember this so you can appreciate the significance of worth.

There are a million different claims made about how dangerous using is. Spending other people's money can be quite difficult if done carelessly.

For example, you buy a rental property with a variable rate advance. The property is productive and earns a goodrevenue at first. However, the premium rate suddenly soars, and there is an unexpected rate adjustment. You currently find yourself in a situation where your income is negative, which may be one of several aggravating factors.

Assuming that you use a hard cash advance on a flip is another model. You get the money, which usually comes with a hefty loan fee because it's just a temporary advance, and then the flip task takes a bad turn. For example, the recovery cost increases, and you need help to finish the project. As a result, you can't sell the property for what you had planned, and now the advance result is expected.

That being said, you may significantly reduce the risks associated with using if you know exactly what you're doing and have excellent usage structuring skills.

It makes more sense to obtain a fixed-rate loan rather than a customised rate advance in the case of that investment property. Your using hazards drop significantly if you combine a fixed-rate credit with the property being in a strong development area that can attract quality tenants.

While the advance construction stays the same in the case of flipping a house with actual cash, you must understand the core of what you're doing as a flipper to reduce risk. Flipping properties is a straightforward concept: you buy a distressed home, fix it up, and then sell it for more money than you originally paid. However, there are a lot of challenges involved that new investors may need to be made aware of. The unexpected difficulties may put the financial sponsor at grave risk of being unable to repay that advance. Establishing an emergency strategy for credit restitution ahead of time, in case the flip goes awry, is another way to reduce risk in this scenario.

"»»

It's undeniable that using other people's money to contribute to your portfolio is not only incredibly helpful financially but also frequently necessary to continue expanding your holdings. But in the end, financial success is a relative metric, much like any other kind of advancement. A person's definition of achievement and advancement could be ludicrously different from one another. Some people are quite happy with having small portfolios. There are also those people who may be so uncomfortable using money—that is, using other people's money—that they may believe that no amount of financial success is worth the stress they may put on it. It's not necessary to be extremely creative with money in either of those situations. Nevertheless, you can create the possibility of limitless growth if you do choose to take advantage of the opportunity to use other people's money in your contribution.

Market Structure
What is truly meant to be heard when someone refers to the "stock market" is the global network of stock exchanges. A stock exchange is a physical venue where financial asset buyers and sellers

interact. Situated in New York City on Wall Street, the New York Stock market is the most well-known stock market globally. In the US, here is where the majority of transactions take place. Still, comparable trades occur in Miami, Chicago, and Philadelphia.

In addition, there are numerous stock exchanges globally. Cities around Europe, like London, Paris, Frankfurt, and Madrid, are home to some of the biggest. The Shanghai, Tokyo, and Seoul stock exchanges are the most important ones in Asia. Latin America contains further markets.

In one of these stock exchanges, you trade directly when you purchase and sell stocks, among other assets. It would be best if you familiarise yourself with the many types of assets that are traded in them. Please remember that not all markets will always have the same support. Certain markets focus more on one kind of asset than others. Additionally, businesses have a single exchange listing them. As a result, a firm that is listed in the US is not eligible to be listed abroad. Therefore, you may also need to consider an international market if you are serious about trading a particular company.

Asset Groups
In financial markets, assets other than stocks are exchanged. There are several options available for acquisitions. This book is primarily concerned with stocks. However, the following is a list of the securities available for trading in financial markets:
Government bonds issued by the US and other nations
Commodities (energy, cattle, industrial metals, precious metals, and agricultural items)
Currencies: any global currency
Exchange-traded funds, swaps, and options
Mutual, index, and exchange-traded funds
Certain assets, like bonds, are ideal for a "buy and hold" approach, while other assets, like commodities, are better suited for short-term investments. In the

end, your expectations and objectives will determine which of these asset classes you invest in.

We advise utilising stock initially. Prior to pursuing other asset classes, it is the ideal technique to get started. Before diving into other asset classes, it's crucial to become an expert in stock trading, as certain transactions demand more knowledge and research. Still, investing across a range of asset classes allows you to create a diversified portfolio. In particular, diversification is an excellent tactic to safeguard against long-term risk.

1.5 Markets: Bull and Bear

Bull markets are characterised by sustained and notable market growth. Markets that have experienced substantial, prolonged declines are referred to as bear markets. Every one of them has benefits and drawbacks.

1.5.1 An explanation of bull markets

supply is exceeding demand, investor confidence is high, and prices are rising. In the event that prices in a particular market are rising quickly, it may indicate that a growing number of shareholders are becoming "bullish" about future price increases and that a bull market is about to begin.

A positive feedback loop that increases investor confidence draws in more capital and raises prices.

Since the level of public trust in a cryptocurrency affects its price significantly, some investors look for indicators of investor optimism in the market (referred to as "market sentiment" metrics).

1.2.52 What are the telltale signals of an end to a bull market?

There will inevitably be ups and downs, dips, and corrections in a bull market. It's possible to misinterpret brief price drops as the conclusion of the bull market. Because of this, it's imperative to consider any potential indications of a trend reversal in a broader perspective and analyse price movement over longer timeframes.

Bull markets are short-lived, and investor confidence will eventually decline. A number of factors, including negative news or unexpected events like the COVID-19 pandemic, may contribute to this decline. A substantial negative price movement may indicate the onset of a bear market, in which an increasing number of traders believe that shares will continue to fall, which will cause a downward spiral as they sell to cover their losses.

Rates are falling, optimism is low, and supply outweighs demand. Hence, investors who are negative and believe that prices will keep falling are referred to as "bears." Bear market trading can be challenging, particularly for inexperienced traders.

When a bear market ends, and the lowest price is reached, it is notoriously hard to predict because the recovery is frequently a slow, erratic process influenced by a range of outside factors, such as investor psychology, economic growth, and world news or events.

But they could also present opportunities. Furthermore, investing during a low market could pay you handsomely when the cycle turns around if you have a longer-term investment plan. Investors using shorter-term techniques must be alert for price escalation or regression. For more experienced investors, there are further strategies, including brief selling, which is speculating on an asset's price decline. Dollar-cost averaging, which involves spending a specific amount of money (let's say $50) every week or month, regardless of whether the asset's value is rising or falling, is another strategy used by many cryptocurrency investors. By doing this, you can invest in both up and down markets and spread your risk.

Getting By In The New Economy And Growing

SO, WHAT TAKEN PLACE?

"Toto, I don't think we're still in Kansas." In the excellent film The Wizard of Oz, Dorothy made a great statement. It is a different country, a different economy, and a new battlefield where all of the previous rules no longer apply. This "new typical" and reset happen during every business cycle, as was previously mentioned.

The problem for the majority of Americans is that they will continue to behave, labour, and make contributions as if the previous standard still needed to be revised. This effort will be similar to rowing upstream in that it will be very challenging to gain any ground and very easy to lose ground if the rowing isn't 100% productive. How long can someone maintain that level of work?

People may easily make decisions and designs that will enable them to paddle with the current if they have even a rudimentary understanding of the fundamentals of our New Economy and the interventionist plans of our administration and the Federal Reserve.

Our government needs money, a lot of it. Moreover, the degree of requirement will continue to rise. The problem isn't going away; in actuality, it's only going to grow worse.

"Our government needs money. Our politicians need to be made aware of fiscal restraints.

Substantially increasing the total debt accumulated during the first 237 years of our nation's existence!

The CARES Act, the largest financial improvement in our country's history, was enacted in response to the 2020 COVID-19 epidemic, which resulted in a government shutdown. This slump has once again necessitated bailout "help" in the form of trillions of additional dollars into the economy. The Department of the Treasury and the Federal Reserve came up with a scheme that essentially handed the Treasury over to the Fed's printing press. Our Federal Reserve is free to print as much money as it likes, provided that it does so cautiously, as our currency is currently not tied to a gold-backed standard. This "bandaid improvement" is an additional duty that pushes the burden of obligation repayment onto subsequent generations.

Unfortunately, there will inevitably be more problems than the Federal Reserve and the Treasury can solve as a result of their convergence (unseen side-effects). In essence, it increases the authority of the Federal Reserve. It will likely be used to allow the central government to purchase resources such as business equity and financial institutions that it is not really entitled to.

What happens if a President—whether the one in office now, the one next, or the one before that—needs to nationalise the private sector? What happens if a president decides that the government must regulate housing, manufacturing, or the financial industry, orders the Treasury to buy up pieces of those companies, and directs the Fed to finance the purchase? What effects have the "takeover" of the medical services sector by public authorities had?

This is a disgrace to the free-enterprise foundation upon which our country was built—not as the perfect financial system, but rather as the greatest the world has ever seen. This will lead to further governmental corruption and takeover of the commercial sector—what some may refer to as "socialism."

This grants the President unrestricted authority, allowing him to directly influence the financial decisions made by the Fed and the Treasury's purchase decisions.

The flute player ought to get paid eventually. Where does this money end up? Banks held a large portion of it during the recent financial crisis, which allows them to credit the money back to the Federal Reserve on a predetermined total revenue basis with absolutely no risk to the institutions.

The banks need more incentive to be assertive in lending cash to businesses and clients because they are typically restricted by the public authority and mostly reliant on administrative tools maintained after the 2008 financial crisis. When banks finally do offer these kinds of loans, only some businesses and purchasers are able or desire to go through the approach because the guaranteeing system has grown so complex and demanding.

China, Japan, and the Saudis currently bear a large portion of the nation's debt. As a result of the Federal

Reserve's plans to generate more money, our dollar is becoming less valuable. Eventually, these holders of new obligations will "bring in their notes," or demand higher lending costs to make up for the dollar's decreased purchasing power.

A mere increase in finance expenses, equivalent to one or two percentage points, will have catastrophic effects on our economy. But this will only last for a while. When interest rates rise, the premium payments on our ever-growing public debt will draw more money out of the economy and be needed for an unrelenting administration.

What is Not Investing

It is necessary to examine what investing is not in order to comprehend better what it is. Graham's definition is useful in this case since it provides us with a key indicator of what to look for. You should base your investment decisions on items that can be verified and have a track record of performance since investing operations are sophisticated and have a high chance of success. Furthermore, as this is what turns the odds in your favour, how well your tactics are executed is crucial (Palmer, 2019).

It is evident from reading any stock investing blog or Twitter account that most people switch between topics frequently. They buy in bitcoin the next day, and Tesla calls the day before that. Some even succeed in making money by doing this.

Money is a useful criterion to assess a strategy's effectiveness, but it's far more crucial to look at the strategy's scalability and repeatability. Reliability is easy to comprehend. How frequently can you use the same approach and get the same outcomes? Many opportunities depend on unique circumstances that might not arise again.

For instance, when the pandemic struck, hedge fund manager Bill Ackman gained a billion dollars by betting against the US stock market. He was able to capitalise on a unique set of circumstances—a worldwide pandemic that was enacting lockdowns everywhere and that the US administration at the time was choosing to overlook. International precedent had been established, and he could easily understand how the lockdowns would affect the United States. This was not an investing plan, despite being extremely profitable. How much longer till the identical set of circumstances arises again? You never know when they might show up and how you might be able to take advantage of them.

We refer to these tactics as "speculation." Graham saw firsthand how speculation led to the stock market disaster that preceded the Great Depression; he was adamantly against it. His viewpoint is very extreme, though, and there is no disputing that speculating can be a very profitable endeavour. All it takes is a great deal more effort (Bogle, 2017).

Speculators never have the same opportunity twice, and they have to come up with new ideas all the time. Sadly, most conjecture is dumb. Only the most astute can thoroughly examine a set of conditions and calculate their chances of success. These speculators really take the form of "investors" on WallStreetBets (WSB) or other similar social media platforms.

These guys only depend on luck to make money; they have yet to learn what they are doing. Their tactics are absurd, and they are too ignorant to recognise this, such as inflating the stocks of insolvent companies to damage "hedge funds" while enriching hedge funds greatly. Everyone follows suit as someone provides a screenshot showing how they made over $100,000 purchasing AMC shares.

Excessive emotions and hysteria are characteristics of illogical speculation. Traders and investors who are successful do not brag about what the market is doing. Rather, they discreetly carry out their daily activities and assess the situation for themselves.

Speculation has little chance of success, intelligent or not. First of all, this is due to the significant influence that luck has on how events transpire. Secondly, you have to continuously seek out new chances because the tactics you select are not replicable. It is complex to accomplish this.

Finally, many chances that are speculative need to be more scalable. Scalability is a factor that most investors overlook. A $1,000 technique might be quite successful, but if you invest

$10,000 in it, it might not work at all. Something that functions well with $10,000 might function poorly with $1 million.

Investment techniques are scalable, meaning that no matter how much money is invested, the return is guaranteed. They also do not require an investor to look for brilliant ideas because they are very repeatable continuously. As such, all it takes for investors to become extremely wealthy is a small number of brilliant ideas.

A BUSINESS'S VALUE: WHAT IS IT?

Only when the price we pay today is significantly less than the value we will receive tomorrow will we invest in a company? Example: A teacher picks up a student at the row. The teacher hands the pupil a $10 bill and inquires, "What is the value of this bill?" 10 dollars. The teacher picks up ten $1 bills. She asks, "What is the value of these dollar bills?" repeatedly. Ten cents. The teacher offers to exchange the ten $1 bills for the $10 bill from the pupil. This is a risk so he may take it or he will not.

Subsequently, the teacher proposes to exchange the $10 for just five $1 bills. Naturally, he ought to accept it. Ask the remaining participants, "How many of you would buy this?" at a large scale. ACT in reverse. Will you accept ten $1 bills in exchange for the $10 bill? What number would take this? None at all.

When the market only offers $5 for $10 bills, the best investors can easily steal them. However, how is this possible? It is possible because 1) the value is easy to calculate, and 2) the market needs to be more logical.

Remember that the market gets crazy. Is this anything you find good or bad? It is really a good thing. Making money in the stock market would be extremely challenging if all investors based their choices on conservative and realistic estimates of intrinsic value. Thankfully, the participants in the stock market are human and susceptible to the correlating influence of emotions. Many investors will become hysterical over stocks, or people will follow a trend, believing that they can outperform the system. As youthful investors, we always check emotions at the door and purchase stocks based on what they are truly worth.

However, how can we determine the company's worth?

Let us use the App. What is the value of the largest consumer electronics market in the world? Any business's value is equal to the present value of all future cash flows, less the amount of money required for investments to make this happen. Alright, that was intense. Bear with me.

Let us assume that today, Every year, Apple sells 200 million products at an average price of $1,000. Thus, they earn $200 billion in sales annually. However, they had to spend $700 per gadget to design and manufacture them, plus an additional $100 to purchase the equipment, in order to produce those 200 million goods. Thus, they are bringing home $200 for each device or forty billion dollars. Next year, would you be willing to exchange $40 for $40? No, not unless you believe that Apple will continue to make money in the upcoming year. All right, let us assume that Ample sells 5% more products annually at the same $1,000 price. They make $44 billion the following year, $48.4 billion the year after, and so forth. Then, Apple's value becomes everything below the surface. Let us hope Apple can continue this trend for the ensuing forty years. The total amount of profits going forward is currently valued at approximately $675 billion. Not bad, huh? After dividing that figure by the total number of shares outstanding, we arrive at an approximate share value of USD 111.

2.2.1. What "Unbanked" Means.

What does being unbanked entail? 2.5 billion people who live in real money-based social orders and have no access to financial services are classified as unbanked by the World Bank. Helpfully, they only count heads of household.

Only the necessary workers matter in this estimation; spouses and children are irrelevant. However, we acknowledge that women limit daily family finances in the vast majority of the world. They are not, however, regarded as the head of the household.

To be unbanked is not to only dwell in a money-driven society. To be unbanked is to need availability to the world, not to have the capability to take part in exchange and trade, not to be able to discover a new line of work and find individuals who need your administration. To be unbanked is to strive to build a safer future for your children. It is to be sentenced to poverty. When we check out those conditions, we figure, 'They do not have cash, that is the reason they're unbanked.' Wrong. Totally off-base. They do not approach documentation or the essential ability to fill in an application form.

Sometimes, they do not have the clothing, shoes, or appearance to have the choice to enter a bank without being kicked out by a safety officer. That is being unbanked.

2.2.2. The Price of Exclusion from Finance

How much does financial avoidance cost? Massive destitution is caused all throughout the world to ensure that we can maintain this little, shared belief that, as long as each participant exhibits morality, we can track every conversation through this framework of reconnaissance and put an end to wrongdoing. Through our belief in the false notion of well-being via authoritarian rule, we condemn billions of people to poverty. 2.5 billion, but a great many more.

We discuss financial considerations from the vantage point of our diverse and unique world. The environment I am in. I can open a bank account since I live in America, but I can also freely swap other currencies and take advantage of investment opportunities all across the world. I move towards stable financial structures that will not collapse in the near future and take all of my reserve money with them. I approach foundations that, more often than not, will either not be able to process my money efficiently or will swiftly destroy it in order to satisfy their commitment through unchecked inflation, causing financial collapse. How many people are in possession of that? Probably everyone in this room.

However, if you include everyone on the earth who has access to that level of financial administration, that number may be as high as 1.5 billion. That is why, after 2013, I started announcing loudly and unambiguously, "This is about the other six billion." That is what it means to consider money.

Our administrative structure is preventing people from accessing financial services. We have reached a stage when being allowed access to basic financial services has become advantageous. To be granted the benefit of financial administrations, the average person must dance to prove to an investor that they are admirable, filling out endless forms and desk labour. We are even criticising currency, the ultimate anonymous, fungible, peer-to-peer mechanism that has given everyone access to basic financial services for millennia.

Value of Time

The entire amount by which the option price exceeds the intrinsic option value is the time value, sometimes referred to as the extrinsic value. It is closely related to the total time remaining before the expiration date of any option. The time value of an option's formula is quite simple to calculate:

Price of option - intrinsic value equals time value.

Any option's chances of ending up in the money increase with the amount of time it has left until its expiration date. Any option's time component tends to deteriorate progressively. In reality, the option time value's derivative is a complicated equation. It is generally the case that an option will lose one-third of its value in the first half of its life and two-thirds in the second. This is a crucial component for investors in securities since the closer the expiration date, the more change in the price of the underlying assets will be required to affect the option price.

Market volatility affects an option's time value as well. The time value of an option is typically quite low for stocks that are not anticipated to move substantially. The time value of the option will typically be minimal for all those equities that are not anticipated to move substantially. For the more erratic stocks, the inverse is likewise true.

Unpredictability

Most of the time, assessing the overall effect of volatility is challenging and subjective. Today, many different kinds of calculators can be used to determine the anticipated volatility. When working with options trading, you are likely to encounter a variety of volatility kinds. Historical volatility, or HV, is useful in estimating the potential size of any underlying stock's future movements. Within a certain time frame, two-thirds of all conceivable events involving a stock's price will occur within one standard deviation move, either positive or negative. HV is used to illustrate how erratic a market can be.

Implied volatility is calculated using the market's current prices and is frequently utilised in conjunction with theoretical models. Setting the current price of any available choice is greatly aided by it. It also aids option players in accurately evaluating the trade possibilities. An options trader can estimate future volatility by using implied volatility. But, it can reveal the current mood of the options market. This attitude will then be directly reflected in the option price, assisting traders in estimating future option volatility and stock price based solely on current option prices.

Understanding the entire process of how options are priced is essential for any stock investor who is serious about using up options to capitalise on the possible nature of movement in a given stock. , whether it be up or down, must have a thorough understanding of both the current and anticipated volatility in the options price.

Additional Things To Think About

When Investing

Recognise real estate laws.
The law controls every facet of real estate. Real estate transactions entail several stakeholders and intricate legal considerations.

The contract is by far the most important factor when buying or selling real estate. The primary objective of a contract is to record, in writing, the mutual consent—that is, the agreement of both parties to the transaction. Legal enforcement is not available for verbal agreements. For a contract to be deemed valid, it must contain the following components:

The names of the parties concerned and the amount that was agreed upon

Any specific "consideration" that is being given in exchange, usually money, needs to be stated.

The signatures of each person concerned

People are always protected by checks and balances that also protect the larger system. The purpose of appraisals is to ensure that the property is worth the sum that the seller and lender have claimed. The assessment forbids investors and mortgage brokers from engaging in dishonest business dealings. There are certain guidelines for the use and sale of commercial real estate. There are regulations in place to safeguard the landlord and the tenants if the property is rented out. The law holds lenders responsible for determining the maximum amount they can lend, what paperwork and insurance are required, and even how they advertise their lending initiatives.

Since tax law has a big impact on your real estate investing performance, you must comprehend it or seek professional advice. Making mistakes may be expensive; therefore, by safeguarding yourself, you can decide in a way that will increase rather than decrease your profit margin.

Establish a fantastic team and lead with strength.

A company's success is frequently the result of the efforts of every employee. More than employee talent and skill is needed to guarantee success. There is another equally vital item. This is what gathers all the talent and energy in order to focus it on a particular objective. This is what will create a fantastic team that outperforms its rivals on a regular basis. Any team, whether it be a corporation or a school class, needs strong and dependable leadership. Even if the team consists of excellent individuals, a leader still needs to get everyone on board and work together amicably. A handful of exceptionally talented professional sports teams never make it to the postseason.

Much writing has been done on leadership. Nonetheless, a leader's dedication to the business, team, or common objective is the essence of leadership. This pledge inspires others to do the same. Individuals who are personally committed are more likely to make the correct decisions, endure, and follow through until their objectives are met. A leader's dedication binds the team's ideas and perspectives together, making the total larger than the sum of its parts. Positive outcomes are possible even from unconscious activities. Personal dedication also fosters trust—the belief that the team's efforts will produce the best outcomes—between the leader and the members of the team. It is easy. Could you give it some thought? Even if they may respect someone else's intelligence, individuals sometimes get the impression that they do not care for them. The majority of people will not follow someone they do not trust, real or not.

Although there are many different kinds of leaders, all of them are dedicated to a cause, an organisation, or an objective. To be able to endure through trying times, this is necessary. Their followers begin to trust them because of their clear commitment. To lead them is the purpose of the leader. They imitate the leader's actions. Leaders who take ownership of their team's tragedies will instil trust in them.

Gaining An Edge in a Bear Market

Bear markets are not growing quickly and have recently been less healthy generally. A bear market is one in which the market has dropped by 20% or more over a year. These kinds of market situations have also occurred, but none are as recent in our memories as the financial crisis of 2008. During this time, all businesses were concerned about their future. Even in cases where the business was performing well and had little to do with the previous year's housing crisis, investors were withdrawing their money out of businesses due to anxiety. It is still possible to invest during a bear market, and if you want to do so for the rest of your life, you probably will. The stock market will only sometimes be doing well, and it can even remain stagnant for a while. You can still perform well for yourself using short-term positioning, regardless of the circumstances.

In a down market, short selling is the most obvious tactic. Selling shares for a stock you do not own with the goal of buying it when the price decreases to a specific level is known as short selling. Assume for the moment that the stock of fictional business XYZ, which is now trading at $70, is overpriced. The stock price will drop one day, and you want to make money off of their losses. You might acquire shares at a lower price by setting a short sell; the stock must reach this price in order for the option to take effect and for you to be able to buy it at the new, lower price. Suppose you determine it will reach $50. In this instance, you will pay $50 for the shares and profit $20 on each share.

Even now, short selling may still appear like a hazardous strategy, and it does need work on the investor's behalf.

Knowing which stock to short and having enough confidence in it to hit your desired price are prerequisites. You may not be able to commit this kind of time. In a bear market, your concerns are more focused on the companies you already own than on the ones you wish to acquire. To guarantee your right to sell your shares at a specific price in this situation, you can buy a put option. In this instance, let us pretend that ABC Company employs you.

You have received excellent treatment from ABC throughout the years, and you have a sizable stake in the business. There is no denying that the market is about to tank, and you have no idea what to do. There is a lot to think about and a lot at risk here. What does it mean to dump stock if you do not believe in the company? Also, what about the savings you committed to this investment? Even if the business appears to be doing well, you have the uneasy feeling that you should not be selling at this particular time. You are effectively building a little cushion and protecting yourself so that you can sell at $75 regardless of what happens to the firm if the stock is trading at $80 and you receive a put option to sell at $75. This is less than the $80 you could have sold it at previously, but you avoided losing as much money and were able to hold onto the stock rather than risking everything at the moment you wanted to sell it at $80. The premium on the option is the cost associated with having the right to the option's strike price, how long the option is available, etc. However, this implies that you have the freedom to design your own unique insurance plan and pay a fee to maintain it. This is an excellent tactic if you have less time to keep an eye on the market or if you do not know what the future holds. Yes, there is a cost, but keep in mind that by holding onto your stock and purchasing the put option's peace of mind, you can escape potentially significant losses.

A short exchange-traded fund, or ETF, is an additional option for a time-constrained investor. You are effectively betting on unfavourable outcomes, much like with a short position, except you are investing against an index rather than an individual firm. Since an index is a collection of funds, you can wager against whole industries with an exchange-traded fund (ETF). Because you are betting on an industry-wide trend rather than just the earnings of a single firm that might turn out to be an exception, using this option can yield far higher returns than taking a single short position. It is also slightly safer. In this instance, an ETF will increase in percentage terms in response to a few percentage point decline in the index. This can also be thought of as searching for a decreasing slope inside a narrow segment of the advance/decline line for the stock market. Similar to an advance/decline line for a select few companies, an index is a bet on a ratio that, on average, results in a slope that is less than 1.

Develop. Home

GROW.HOUSE presented itself amid a recent breakup with Burton. As the "first-ever digital meetup for fans of cannabis, cryptocurrency, and decentralised finance." Imagine Farmville and Robotron but with cannabis as the primary edible crop traded in cryptocurrency. Under the direction of brand guru Brendan Hampton, who famously created a fake Dave Chappelle Twitter account, the game was developed on the Polygon network and enables users to grow edible cannabis, earn $GROW tokens, buy NFTs, and gain knowledge about yield farming. The company, which made its first public offering (IDO) on June 1, has received funding from Polygon, Ave, Soulja Boy, JuÈcy Fields, and other sources. When the GROW.HOUSE marketplace launches, users will be able to purchase convertible NFTs and other assets.

● Location: MamÈ ● Category: Video games, television

Zeptagram, established in St. Clark by Chrystina and Johann ForsmanLöwenŕtröm, enables musicians to turn their tracks into NFTs and offer a portion of the ownership rights to enthusiasts and investors. During the second-hand sale, muĕicians and their supporters receive rewards through astute contracts. The company has created its cryptocurrency, Zeptacoin, which is utilised for exchanging music rights on the platform and paying for royalties. A CRowdsalecampaign, which is presently {olding artists such as MelĖshaLinnell, Wylie LĖgomeka, and TauraiMudamburi as proprietorship shares in the marketplace.

● Location: Sweden's Stockholm
● Category: Audio, artwork, games, photography, video

Valuables
Through a platform developed by Cent, Values, users can auction off their Twitter followers in exchange for cash.

Buyers can submit bids by entering the user's handle or the Twitter URL in a search bar. Minimum bids begin at $1 unless the vendor has specified a reserve price. This is the location where Jack Dorsey, the CEO of Twitter, famously sold his autographed first tweet for $2.9 million.

● Location: San Francisco
● Category: Twitter

NFT Trading: What do NBA cards, Nyan Cat, and the first -ever tweeter have in common? IFT. As soon as everyone started to get into the blockchain craze, NFT trading jumped in and contributed fuel to an already massive fire. This tutorial will teach you how to purchase and sell NFTs, as well as which NFT markets are the best.

NFTs are available in various shapes and sizes, offering lucrative opportunities for collectors and artists alike. You might be thinking how profitable NFT trading is if the price of a pop-tart cat from ten years ago is worth a mention. roughly $70-

million. That is the amount that a Beeple digital art piece was sold for at the beginning of 2021. If you were intrigued, read the entire article to discover everything there is to know about NFTs, including how they operate and how to start trading them.

Due to the lengthy history of US stock markets, US investors frequently have the greatest impact. Currently, most nations allow citizens to invest in stock markets. Here are five well-known investors that you might look into more to pick the brains of the greatest:

Bogle, John (Jack)

This individual is largely responsible for the low-cost Exchange Traded Funds (ETFs) that provide investors access to whole markets for little to no additional cost.

Bogle invented the Vanguard 500, a low-cost index fund. This charges investors a small fee and performs similarly to the S&P 500. From these modest beginnings, exchange-traded funds (ETFs) have proliferated and become a safer option for novice investors.

Bogle offered eight investment guidelines:

Select inexpensive funds.

Purchase and hold onto a fund portfolio.

Avoid having too many assets.

Watch out for celebrity managers.

Particularly, large assets should be monitored.

Analyse prior results to determine risk.

A fund may not perform as well as it did in the past just because of its past performance.

Make sure you receive a good value for your money if you are paying for an actively managed fund.

Buffett, Warren

The "Omaha Oracle" Buffett is the ideal investor for everyone. He began investing with £174k and made about £100 billion out of it.

Buffett acquired Berkshire Hathaway, a company that made textiles, in 1965. He made it a holding company for investments in industrial, energy, and insurance companies. Buffett has avoided investing in technology; he only makes investments in industries he is familiar with, and novice investors would be well to emulate him.

Buffett is in a better position than novice investors. The fact that he intervened in businesses he had invested in is one of his numerous success stories. Because of his ownership stakes, he had the power to impose structural and managerial reforms that helped turn around businesses.

The Snowball: Warren Buffett and the Business of Life, Buffett's biography, has all the details.

Flipping Houses: The Second Season

In a little Arkansas town, Doug met a woman who was hoping to move back home but was only planning to stay a week. After being given a tour of the property, Doug observed that it was a modest house with well-kept landscaping. It was quite another tale on the inside, however.

Doug assured the woman that he would take her asking price of $30,000 back to his partner to see what could be done after seeing the house. Doug, however, committed to give her $10,000 within thirty days with his partner.

Doug and his business partner then swiftly turned the house around and sold it to a different buyer at a higher asking price.

Earnings are strong:

A little house, around 2,000 square feet, that had been completely renovated was bought by Rick and his partner. After a significant amount of work and roughly six months, they were done.

They had invested $50,000 on the property and another $90,000 in repairs for the house.

They were able to work out a deal for about $19,000 less than what they had been asking after trying to sell the house to recover their investment. However, before it could be finished, the deal collapsed.

After they kept the house on show and had no bites, they went to a professional.

They were successful in negotiating a comparatively low fee that was split between the listing agent and the agent by using a reputable real estate company. They received an offer a few weeks later that was over $2,000 less than what they had requested.

By completing the deal, they were able to get paid. After all expenses were covered, they ultimately turned a profit.

They have now finished a number of other projects, all of which turned a profit!

The lesson from the anecdote is that because you are selling a property and assisting someone, you will probably make money regardless of who you deal with or how you market the property.

You will ultimately forfeit your investment and incur losses if you give up on your endeavours. If, at first, you are not getting what you want, hang in there and do not give up. Investing a few times could be necessary before you get what you want.

Make sure you are able to work out a deal with someone who really wants the house without losing too much ground.

You are giving someone a house that they may have been looking for for a long time in addition to putting money in your pocket. You are helping a person! Isn't that incredible?

What Goals Do Investments Have?

It is important to understand the goals of the speculation and its meaning before deciding to invest your money in any of the many growth techniques available in India. The general goals of setting aside money could be any of the preceding causes, even though the specific destinations of speculation might change from one financial backer to the next.
Reasons to Begin Investing Right Now: 1. To Protect Your Money

For people, one of the most important goals of their ventures is capital conservation. Some conjectures aid in preventing hard-earned money from dissipating over time. You can ensure that your investment funds do not outlive you by stopping your assets in these programmes or instruments. A regular bank account, fixed stores, and government securities can all help to safeguard your money. Even though there may be less profit to be made, capital protection is easily achieved.

2. To Promote Money Gains

Making sure that money grows into a substantial corpus over time is another common goal of storing money. Most The most effective endeavours to achieve development involve property, common assets, goods, and value. These decisions may carry a great risk, but they also frequently have a large reward.

3. To generate a stable flow of income

Additionally, you can use speculations to help you find a reliable source of additional (or necessary) income. Examples of such businesses include fixed outlets that pay regular premiums or suppliers of companies that consistently provide financial supporters with revenues. After your resignation, pay-creating guesses can help you cover your ongoing expenses. However, they can also serve as excellent sources of income during your long career by providing you with additional funds to cover expenses such as EMIs or school fees.

4. To reduce the Tax Burden

Financial investors have other compelling goals for the venture in addition to capital expansion or conservation. The Income Tax Act of 1961's tax cutbacks served as the source of this motivation. Investing in options such as Public Provident Funds (PPF), Equity Linked Savings Schemes (ELSS), and Unit Linked Insurance Plans (ULIPs) may require deductions from your take-home pay. As a result, your available salary is reduced, which lessens your need to cover expenses.

5. To build retirement funds

It is necessary to set aside money for retirement. Since you will only be able to work for a while, it is essential to establish a retirement account that you can vouch for in your prime. You can allow your assets to grow to the point where they can sustain you after you have quit by investing the money you earn throughout your career in wise investments.

6. To reach your financial objectives

Contributing can also help you reach your financial goals, both short- and long-term, without putting too much strain or trouble on you. Certain venture options, for instance, come with high liquidity and brief lock-in periods. These businesses are great ways to avoid using your assets if you want to lay aside money for short-term goals like building a secret stash or paying for house improvements. Other options for speculation that come with a longer lock-in term are great for putting money aside for future goals.

Steer clear of the hype.

Be extremely sceptical of any new cryptocurrency that is being hailed as the next big thing that you learn about. Frequently, it needs to be clarified if tech media and periodicals are invested in a new coin. This would be dishonest unless the publisher properly disclosed their involvement, if any. Do your research whenever you read or hear about a new coin that is being touted. If you quickly explore the internet, you might discover that the hoopla is real, or it might just be hype.

Furthermore, it will already be too late if your neighbours, barber, or mechanic start telling you about cryptocurrency. Exactly this is what transpired with Bitcoin. The ship had sailed on the genuine gains when common people were swarming to get a piece of the action.

Note that the coins you have yet to hear of are usually the best.

How come?

Well, because they have yet to become well-known or traction. This is frequently because they have yet to be tested in real-world situations. Therefore, until inventors are certain that their coin—or blockchain, for that matter—works in practice, they don't advertise it. That is the reason they will be really low initially. Investors will see this as a chance and seize it in the hopes that it will soar. The loss would not be too great if the coin were to fall flat.

Begin with a tiny
It is generally best to start small when investing for the first time. Starting modestly could entail investing $100 in a number of inexpensive coins. Certain coins are worth about the same as pennies for every dollar. These, however, could be overpriced and offer very little benefit.

Next, some coins are exchanged for a few dollars each. These have a decent chance of being profitable because they could see large dollar gains. Now, it is advisable to avoid expensive products like Bitcoin, Litecoin, or Ethereum, whether you get super cheap coins or not. For example, Litecoin can cost you roughly $200 per coin. In the beginning, this could be too much to handle. When you have more experience, you may spend at this level with confidence. This is because of your familiarity with the industry and your knowledge of it. Upon gaining familiarity with the market's trajectory, you can proceed to place larger bets with assurance.

Do not be scared to take part in something.

In the cryptocurrency world, Bitcoin remains supreme. Only a few people, meanwhile, have $5,000 to invest in a single Bitcoin. Thus, you may research exchange-traded funds (ETFs) or alternative cryptocurrency funds that provide you with the opportunity to purchase a portion of a Bitcoin. Even while you would never truly possess the coin, you would still be exposed to the market. This implies that you would benefit according to the investment you have in a coin if the price action rises higher.

Funds of this kind are available for expensive assets like gold or real estate. Once you invest in the fund, you become a part owner. If you put in enough money, you can buy the asset outright. However, the majority of investors do not truly wish to possess the actual object. All they desire is market visibility and, consequently, the associated profits. Therefore, spend some time researching the terms of partial cryptocurrency ownership that your broker can provide you.